The Funny Side of

VICTORIA WOOD

The Funny Side of

....

VICTORIA
WOOD

Bruce Dessau

First published in 1997 by Orion Media
an imprint of Orion Books Ltd
Orion House, 5 Upper St Martin's Lane, London WC2H 9EA

Copyright © Orion Books Ltd

Designed and created by The Bridgewater Book Company Ltd

A CIP catalogue record for this book is available from the British Library

ISBN 0752810154

Colour reproduction by Pixel Colour Ltd London
Printed and bound in Great Britain
by Butler & Tanner Ltd, Frome and London

Contents

'Not so Much a Complexion – More of a Doily'

The best comedians stand alone. They arrive at that place called Stardom fully formed. They don't seem to have any historical baggage, they are not strict adherents to any legacy. They don't come trailing a long line of show business antecedents. They are famous and funny in their own right.

Victoria Wood is one of those transcendental comedians. Seeing her on-stage now you might think of Dawn French or Jo Brand or Mrs Merton. You might even think she is not that original. But think back to the 1970s when Victoria Wood first emerged. There was no one else like her. It has become a cliché in popular culture that when someone is a success, the commentators trot out the old chestnut, 'If so-and-so didn't exist we would have had to invent her.' Victoria Wood wasn't the result of focus groups, market researchers and accountants-turned-television producers hunting for a gap in the comedy market. She is her own creation. Not a professional northerner. Not a women's comedian. Simply one of the sharpest observers of the absurdity of life and language in Britain today.

OPPOSITE:
Dripping with cheap jewels and wit: Victoria Wood finds her El Dorado.

On the other hand, like one of Victoria Wood's characters, nothing is that simple. If you look hard enough, there are some forebears. Some boast a closer resemblance than you might actually think. Victoria Wood isn't even the first Victoria Wood to tread the boards with a repertoire of rude stories and naughty songs. In the early part of the century there was Matilda Alice Victoria Wood, a singer of national repute long before television, radio and video sales. She could pack out theatres from Shepherd's Bush in the west of London to the Hackney Empire in the east, with comical ditties such as *Oh Mr Porter* and *One Of The Ruins Cromwell Knocked About A Bit*. Like the later Wood, she was loveable but no sex symbol – her larger-than-life brassiness made her a celebrity in her thirties, adored by men and women of all classes and ages. In those music hall days she was the nearest thing to a superstar. She was better known by her stage name of Marie Lloyd.

Marie Lloyd however was long gone by the time her namesake came along. This Victoria Wood was born on 19 May 1953 in Prestwich, Manchester. Her father, Stanley, was in insurance, selling policies to support his wife and four children.

'I wasn't unpopular, just not needed by anybody'

LEFT:
In her mid '80s uniform of jacket and tie.

OPPOSITE:
With her *Pat and Margaret* co-stars Duncan Preston and Thora Hird.

Victoria had two older sisters, Penelope and Rosalind and a much older brother. Stanley had once had musical aspirations but had put them aside to raise his family. He was a jazz pianist and after work would pull out sheet music and entertain his family. He also had dreams of being a writer. In his later years, when the children had left home and he had time on his hands at last, he would write a play called *Clogs* about life in the north.

'I don't think you could get the pill in Bury. You were lucky if you could get yoghurt'

Victoria Wood's early years were spent in Ramsbottom, a Mancunian outpost near to Bury with a coincidentally comic name. By all accounts it was a contented household, if not one where laughter constantly rang out. But comedy was there. She can still remember going on a family outing to Buxton at the age of six to see Joyce Grenfell. After the show, her older sisters went backstage, but she wasn't allowed because she was too young. In one of those memorable moments that is enough to make even the most cynical starstruck, Wood remembers Grenfell coming out of the stage door to find her, asking, 'Is this Vicky?' The 'jolly hockey sticks' comic left an indelible impression on Wood, one that would shape her life. She also remembers her as the boarding house landlady in the 1953 film *Genevieve*, which she seemed to see repeatedly on trips and Sunday School outings. Apart from the music, Grenfell was the only thing about the film she could abide. When she was in her teens and looking for a way to express herself, she thought back to that single woman on-stage with just a piano to guide her.

Grenfell wasn't sexy, she wasn't grotesque. She just told strange, funny stories about quaint middle-class neurotics, who had cats that would happily sit for hours on a windowsill purring through the geraniums and old school chums with plummy names like Wendy Plackett and Lumpy Latimer. Like Wood, Grenfell had an instinctive ear for the peculiar effects that certain words and names have on an audience. She wrote her own material and was a past master at picking up snippets of dialogue overheard in public places. What Grenfell would do for the twin-set and pearls set, Wood would later do for the mushy peas, pie and chips brigade. Both may have seemed cruel at times but their funny voices were always tinged with affection.

OPPOSITE:

Joyce Grenfell: the comic who had the biggest influence on the young Victoria Wood.

When Wood was eleven her mother Helen gained a degree in English and became a schoolteacher. Of her parents, it was definitely Stanley who exerted the greatest influence over Victoria in terms of career. She later joked that her mother is the only woman who doesn't have a sense of humour.

The making of a great comic usually involves the obligatory childhood trauma. Every pearl needs its bit of grit. As the youngest child, Victoria Wood was quite isolated. When she was five her brother, thirteen years her senior, left home to go to university. Wood later recalled that her siblings did push her around and 'sit on her'. She was even made to eat putty. With the arrival of the swinging '60s, things didn't get any easier. Her sisters had turned into elegant young women, while Wood was a rather nondescript teenager – a mixture of greasy hair, spots and glasses. As one of her future characters, condemned to a life sentence working on a chain store make-up counter would say: 'Not so much a complexion – more of a doily.'

At her primary school she had been at the top, rising to the dizzy heights of Biscuit Table Monitor before breezing through her 11-plus. But a place at Bury Grammar School meant that she was now mixing with the *crème de la crème* of Lancashire. Some people thrive on competition. Wood didn't seem to like it and retreated. A feeling of inferiority could be brought on by something as slight as her place on the register. She came last simply because of her surname, but felt sure that in the event of a fire she would be burnt to death as the class left the building in alphabetical order.

LEFT:
Camera-shy but fiercely determined: the tomboy look gets a feminine bob.

Further, sensing that she was neither working class nor 'posh', neither hearty nor horsey, she was in a kind of teenage limbo. It all added to the feeling of being an outsider. In 1980 she was able to get things into perspective in a reflective feature in *Vogue*: 'I wasn't unpopular, just not needed by anybody.'

All of this contributed towards the development of a stubborn streak of rebellion, which would surface occasionally over the next thirty years. It first appeared in a pathological dislike of the grey felt bowler she had to wear for school, but actual misdemeanours followed. As an adult she confessed that she once failed to hand in an essay. To conceal the omission she removed a pile of books from the teacher's desk, so that hers appeared to have been among those that had been taken. She also

ABOVE:
The premier of Victoria's play *Talent* at the Crucible Theatre, Sheffield in 1978. No one else was giving her work so she decided to create some for herself.

did a sponsored walk – very noble – but then pocketed the £13 that she had raised for charity. There were, however, already signs of her future career: when she was thirteen, she wrote a song about a flat-chested girl who took pills to grow her breasts and who harboured a secret desire to be Hattie Jacques.

'You can't write about how popular you've been'

It seemed as if the young Victoria Wood could have quite easily gone right off the rails. She told *Cosmopolitan* that she had been kept behind for so many detentions that her parents thought she was 'on the nightshift'. Only drama kept her close to the straight and narrow. She played Autolycus in a production of Shakespeare's *The Winter's Tale*. It was not a big part, but the school magazine called her 'hilariously roguish'.

At the age of fifteen Wood was clearly going through a typical surly, aggressive phase. A bit of a loner, she even considered becoming a boxer. While others formed gangs she seemed destined to be an outsider. It was the late '60s, a time of permissiveness and adventure, drug experiments and free love, but while others went to discos Victoria Wood stayed in.

Behind the veneer of suburban domesticity there were problems. All adolescents go through a period of shyness, but Wood's was bordering on the acute. Following in the footsteps of her father, she had started to play the piano and the trumpet. Her parents encouraged this and sent her to a male music teacher, but she found herself breaking out in a hot sweat just being in the same room as a man.

Wood's shyness caused her problems in public too. According to some reports, she was once in a cinema when a man started stroking her leg during the film. She was too nervous to stop him or do anything. In October 1989 she talked to *The Times* about being approached by a man in the street who asked her to perform an obscene act. Not unusual experiences for a teenage girl, perhaps, but with Wood's psyche already fragile, these contributed to a growing sense of unease.

Feeling most comfortable at home when no one else was there she would continue to practice the piano, but she was so self-conscious she would only do it when her parents went out. One night, though, they returned early and caught her at the keyboard. They were impressed by what they heard and with their encouragement she started lessons again. But this, in its own way, conspired to put up further

OPPOSITE:
Bitten by the theatre bug: the Rochdale drama enthusiast.

barriers. By now her sisters had left home, and she was the only child at the top of the big suburban house, occupying three rooms, complete with their own piano. She could now spend more and more time on her own. But just when it looked like she might turn into a recluse, the Rochdale Theatre Workshop came to her salvation. She joined and was utterly bitten by the acting bug. She played a prompting wolf in a production of *Dracula*. She was also a prototypical Mrs Overall in a production of *The Rising Generation* by Ann Jellico (with supplementary Doc Martens and false breasts). Years later she would look on the summer of 1968 at the Workshop as the happiest time of her life.

Everything about the theatre drew her in: the role-play, the organisation, even the punishing schedule. She would be the first to arrive in the evenings and the last to leave at night. Suddenly she went from being a virtual loner, never leaving her house, to being ever-present at the youth theatre. It was typical of Wood – a person who never does things by half, whether it is acting, comedy, tidying up or exercise. And there was another attraction at the Workshop. One of the local lads was a boy called Bob Mason. He was a bit of a poet and had won a few writing competitions. They started to go out and 'became an item'.

With Bob, her earlier thoughts of becoming a boxer vanished and a career in entertainment was seriously considered. Combining his way with words with her

LEFT:
Wood's verbal gifts were soon to make her the talk of the drama department.

RIGHT:

**Roger Sloman as
George, Bill Stewart
as Arthur, and
Victoria as Maureen in**
Talent **in 1978.**

musical skills, they started to write songs together. The acorns of a great oak tree of a career were being sown.

As the '60s turned into the '70s everything seemed to be looking up. She even passed some exams and started applying to study drama at university, but she wasn't quite ready to fly away from the nest. One of the first places that she considered was Manchester Poly – a prestigious college for the performing arts that would later send Ben Elton, Rik Mayall and Adrian Edmondson out into the world – but one that wasn't too far from the family home.

In the spring of 1971 Wood travelled into the centre of Manchester for her audition, but during the day was so stricken with nerves she was sick while being taken on a guided tour of the building. The student taking her around tried to cheer her up, talking about the time she had done some nursing and pretending to be a hunched old lady pushing a commode along. This chaperone made a distinct impression on Wood, who couldn't get over how small her eyes were.

Manchester Poly turned down Wood's application, but she did find a place at Birmingham University where she started a degree in drama and theatre arts. This meant leaving home and setting up in bedsit land. It was all a bit of a culture shock for the young northerner, who felt like an ugly duckling once again. Many of the other students, she later recalled, were tall, blonde and willowy and from Hampstead, about as different from Wood as it was possible to be.

Things weren't made any better with the ending of her relationship with Bob Mason. He had gone off to study drama in London and by all accounts had fallen for the only 'tall, blonde and willowy woman from Hampstead' who had decided to stay in London. The final correspondence between them was short and sweet but overflowing with both pathos and humour – two leitmotifs of Wood's professional life. She had been in the middle of putting flares into his jeans when he terminated the relationship, but she insisted on completing the job and sending the trousers on. When he received them he sent her a postcard which, reputedly, simply said: 'Jeans poor work.'

OPPOSITE:

**Wood the Wit:
on-stage in full flow.**

At least being footloose and fancy-free meant that Wood could look into the possibilities of the promiscuity that was sweeping England's campuses in the early '70s. The 'pill' and feminism had helped women acquire a degree of equality in the sexual politics of the day. It was all a bit of a shock to Wood: 'I don't think you could get the pill in Bury. You were lucky if you could get yoghurt.' Unfortunately this coincided with one of Wood's lowest periods. Before Bob Mason she had stayed at home while her peers were snogging at the town disco: now she found herself staying at home while her peers were snogging – and more – at college. Sex seemed so much like part of the curriculum that she once said, 'There was all the worry of making sure you had left the house in clean underwear as well as fretting about pronouncing Chekhov.' She later claimed she was so self-conscious she used to wear her leg-warmers under her trousers. Not surprisingly she felt out of place. She said she 'had delusions of grandeur and ability' and ate her way to happiness. It didn't help that she wasn't having great success in her acting career.

In retrospect, of course, this can all be viewed as part of the obligatory character-building 'comedian's school of hard knocks' from which Wood was destined to graduate with flying colours. The depth of failure would inspire her to great comic heights in later years. As she told the *Sunday Times* in 1982, 'You can't write about how popular you've been.'

As always, every cloud has a silver lining. Wood found increasingly that whenever a play was cast, she would be overlooked. Instead, she was called upon to provide the comic musical interludes during the intervals. It sooned dawned on her that in this role she was probably getting more attention and certainly more laughs. Gradually thoughts of a career as an actress receded and ideas of being a different sort of entertainer crystallised.

Life in Birmingham wasn't all bad. She used to pick up some extra cash working in a bar near the BBC's Pebble Mill studios. One night a group of producers came in. After a few drinks they discovered that she was a musician and invited her to audition. Inevitably, Wood thought this was some kind of joke and didn't take any notice of the invitation. The next day, however, she received a telephone call from the BBC. 'We are here waiting for you to audition. Where are you?' Wood raced

round, played the piano and found herself being booked to do light-entertainment musical turns on the BBC's regional programmes.

'Overnight success' is never literally overnight success of course, and Wood was to prove this axiom more thoroughly than most. She may have had what looked like a blossoming television career before she had even graduated, but things still weren't running smoothly. In 1985 she told Russell Harty that she had entered a talent contest in 1972 and 'lost to a Black and White Minstrel who had snogged her amateurishly in the front of a Ford Prefect.' The course of true love never ran less smoothly than in the front of that Ford Prefect.

The difficulty was that there were few role models for Wood. Apart from Hattie Jacques, who seemed to have cornered the market in fat funny women, Benny Hill's dolly birds were the most popular women in television comedy at the time. But she was getting there. Physical appearances may be superficial but Wood grew her fringe, took to wearing contact lenses and seemed to be gaining confidence. In 1974, spurred on by her provincial success, she decided to enter *New Faces*.

At the time, the television programme rivalled *Opportunity Knocks* as the place where amateur and semi-professional performers could get major exposure and see their careers take off. Wiry redhead Marti Caine was a huge success on the series, showing that a funny woman could go from club stalwart to national sensation in a matter of minutes. When Victoria Wood, physically the opposite of Caine – wide in all the places Caine was narrow, short in all the places Caine was tall, frumpy in all the places Caine was glamorous - heard about auditions taking place in Birmingham she embraced the challenge.

It wasn't that simple. Without a friend working on the programme, Wood might never even have been seen. She jokingly said there were about eight thousand would-be stars at the Dolce Vita nightclub that day, hoping to be auditioned. It was only because her friend put her application at the top of the pile that Wood was even tried out. But it did the trick, she was booked on to the programme and she duly won. It was an auspicious day for comedy in the Midlands: among the 'old people, dwarfs and dodgy singers' another young comic, by the name of Lenny Henry, also got his break that day. And like Wood, he too would have mixed fortunes before he reached the top of his profession.

> **. . . . . . .**
> **'lost to a Black and White Minstrel who had snogged her amateurishly in the front of a Ford Prefect'**
> **. . . . .**

OPPOSITE:

Wood's mirror image Marti Caine. Both found fame on *New Faces*, but for Caine it was instant, for Wood it took somewhat longer.

2

From Dole Queue to Theatrical Cue

A decade later Victoria Wood would describe the
fallout of that fateful New Faces appearance
in one sentence: 'Famous for three
minutes, out of work for two years.' It's a salutary
experience for anyone who thinks they've 'made it'
when they get some TV exposure that New Faces
didn't necessarily help Victoria Wood. It may not
have hindered someone as talented as she, but it
hardly propelled her into the limelight. At least with
hindsight she could make a joke about it: 'My
career didn't so much take off as reverse into the
departure lounge.'

LEFT:
**Wood the
storyteller.**

RIGHT:
**Spread some jam on
your shoes and invite
your trousers
to tea: Wood the
socks symbol.**

LEFT:
**Gracie Fields:
the First Lady
of Lancashire.**

RIGHT:
**Take your pick:
facial humour was
never Wood's forte.**

The problem seemed to be simple: where did a funny songstress, unlike anyone in recent memory, go from there? Wood wasn't the only *New Faces* discovery with problems. Lenny Henry found himself in a similar predicament: where does a black man who does Frank Spencer impressions go from *New Faces*? Henry found himself marooned on *The Black And White Minstrel Show* in the late '70s. You could argue that Victoria Wood's fate was even more cruel. She ended up in a bedsit in Morecambe – a place renowned for nettle beer and old people – with a view over the bus garage.

Wood puts much of the blame for the stalling of her career on the manager who signed her up exclusively while she was rehearsing for the first heat of *New Faces*. She describes him as, 'A barking mad ex-bandleader from Hove who contrived to turn down every offer of work. I suppose he was waiting for the big one, but as far as I was concerned twenty minutes at the West Midlands Women's Institute would have done quite nicely.'

Part of the problem was Wood's own image. She was neither comically ugly nor astonishingly beautiful, simply funny and plain. She had yet to uncover her unique

selling point. Producers would admit she was talented and consider her but would conclude by saying that although she was funny, she didn't fit into the kind of show they were working on. There were female predecessors: apart from Marie Lloyd there had been the variety turns Vesta Victoria, a northern comic from Leeds; Vesta Tilly and Hettie King, each famous for her cross-dressing Burlington Bertie routine and there was Blossom Dearie, with her quirky songs. Gracie Fields, with her comic vocal talents and her 'biggest aspidistra in the world', like Wood, also had Rochdale connections. And more recently there was Libby Morris, a raconteur whose broadcasts had inspired the young Wood.

But it would take a show of the kind which specialised in giving airtime to 'oddballs' such as baritone-bard Jake Thackery or simpering poet Pam Ayres, to give Wood her initial exposure. For two and a half years she signed on, while dreaming of the limo and the tax advisers. Often she would be in her manager's office and overhear him in negotiation. His standard remark to prospective employers, which hardly did anything for her confidence, was 'Fatty's not doing it.' Playing hard to get is one thing, but this was quite ridiculous.

. . . .
'Famous for three
minutes, out of work
for two years.'
. . . .

RIGHT:
Crossing everything
and hoping for success
– it took longer
than expected.

Wood, now in her early twenties, could still be painfully shy. It was revealed in later years that when her manager had typed out her contract, she signed it there and then without reading it because she thought it would have been rude to read it in front of him.

Odd glimmers of work did crop up here and there. She did musical interludes on various radio programmes including *Start The Week*. In an early instance of her distinctive self-deprecating wit she suggested that she had only been given the job so that the rest of the guests could disappear to the toilets for three minutes.

Wood developed a modest reputation for being able to turn out a topical song at short notice. Guy the Gorilla had died? Wood could pay poetic tribute to a monkey. Petrol gone up again? Wood could moan about fuel prices in perfect rhythm. The only trouble was that

'Jake Thackeray with tits'

BELOW:

At the beloved keyboard.

since she didn't read the papers, she sometimes had to be pointed in the right direction, storywise. Even today, her husband goes through her scripts to check that she hasn't unwittingly made a tasteless remark about someone who has just been in the news.

She must have been doing something right though because, eventually, in 1976 she was offered a season on *That's Life*, at that time at the peak of its popularity. Though Wood nearly didn't even get that job. Her manager mentioned he had turned it down and for once Wood was so outraged she reportedly contacted *That's Life* directly and said she wanted the job. After that, she no longer had to introduce herself as a former *New Faces* 'winner', she could call herself 'Jake Thackery with tits'. Even if it didn't open many doors, at least *That's Life* kept her profile up.

Nevertheless, by the age of twenty-three, Victoria Wood thought she was past it. Success had seemed a whisker away, but now it seemed further than ever. The only thing that kept her going was her partner Geoffrey Durham, a large ever-smiling man from Surrey. They met in July 1976 in Leicester at the Phoenix Theatre. He was appearing as Buffalo Bill and she was the show's musical director. At least that's how she described herself – other reports suggest that she was standing in as the pianist for a fortnight, working under the soubriquet of Wilhemina Fifty Fingers, while the regular musician was indisposed. Initially, she had been interested in another man in the company, but he turned out to have been gay. When she first met Geoffrey, he was wearing a wig, a fake tan and a suede jacket. It was love at first sight.

The duo did a summer season in Morecambe and decided they liked it so much they made it their home. Part of the reason might also have been that the DHSS office in Birmingham had finally suggested that she might have to give up looking for work as an entertainer and be prepared to take other work if she wanted to continue to receive benefits. Maybe Morecambe, a seaside town with a showbiz reputation (often used as a dramatic location by Alan Bennett, who called it 'not as common as Blackpool', because people don't enjoy themselves so much there) of sorts, would look more kindly on an entertainer taking up residence there.

As well as an actor, Geoffrey Durham was also a magician, working the clubs as The Great Soprendo – *sorprendo* means 'I astonish' but he left the other 'r' out. He advised Wood on her act and started to motivate her, suggesting she adopt his

. . . .

'I thought *coq au vin* was love in a lorry.'

. . . .

LEFT

During the years of struggle in the late '70s comedy must have seemed like a mug's game, but Wood persevered and the self-belief paid off.

ABOVE:

With Geoffrey Durham, without whom she would have made it, but it wouldn't have been as much fun.

motto: 'I will sit down and make some money every day.' Instead of hunching over the keys, he said she should look at the audience. He also said she should try to rely less on drinking coke and smoking on-stage. And, most importantly, he wasn't afraid to tell her if bits of her act weren't funny.

By the late '70s Wood needed all the advice she could get. Her confidence was at an all-time low. There was a brief tour with musical comic John Dowie, whose angry little ditties included one number called 'I Hate the Dutch'. Despite this vaguely punkish aggression, rock-and-roll mayhem wasn't exactly the order of the day off-stage, but she does remember Dowie fusing a hairdryer in Swansea. At one point she was booked to support Jasper Carrott on tour. It seemed like a good idea at the time: both had musical backgrounds; his audiences, she believed, might appreciate her wit and way with words, too. Unfortunately, she fell victim to the support act's recurring nightmare. Half the audience spent her set in the bar, while the other half were in their seats muttering, 'When is Jasper coming on?' under their breath. At best, you could call it 'a learning experience'.

These tours did help to point to one thing that would become clearer as the years progressed. If Wood was to make a major breakthrough, she would have to do what former folk-singer Billy Connolly had done, and what Jasper Carrott was doing, and put the music on the back burner and concentrate on straight gags. A comical song, however comical, would rarely attain the status of a classic gag. Her songs would always seem to be fillers, giving punters a chance to head for the bar and the toilets. Then again, the music did help to get her noticed by the record-buying public who rarely visited the spoken-word sections.

ABOVE:
Gossip over a cup with a member of her 'family', Celia Imrie.

Gradually, though, work was picking up. Left-wing playwright Dusty Hughes was rather taken by Wood and invited her to contribute to a revue, *In At the Death*, being staged at the Bush Theatre in west London. The theme may have been death, but Wood decided to write something about sex. Her sketch was all about a blonde, nice-but-dim woman who thought she was pregnant although it became clear that she had never even had intercourse.

It was a pivotal moment for a number of reasons. For the first time Victoria Wood found her sketch-writing voice; she hadn't had to hide behind a silly topical song to get a laugh – she could create characters that may have seemed absurd on paper but which when fleshed out were also believable, sympathetic and universal.

OPPOSITE:

**The serious side of
Victoria Wood.**

LEFT:

**Julie Walters:
long-term colleague,
friend and owner of a
very large carrot.**

The other reason this show was memorable was because of the identity of the woman who played the blonde – Julie Walters. She and Victoria Wood had what seemed like an instant rapport until one day, in the cafe over the road while eating liver and peas, Wood realised that they had met before. Julie Walters was the overacting student with tiny eyes who had shown her around Manchester Poly eight years earlier. In fact, the character she had played back in 1970 would return again; those hunched shoulders and pinched cheeks would help to create Mrs Overall in *Acorn Antiques*.

Unwittingly, Victoria Wood was on her way to creating her own repertory company. She had met Celia Imrie while doing *That's Life*; she had even borrowed her dresses. And even before the reunion at the Bush, fate seemed to be pushing the alliteratively entwined Wood and Walters together. A couple of years earlier Wood had applied for a job on Granada Television. She was on the short list of two, but didn't get it. One night when she turned on the programme, Geoffrey remarked that he knew the woman who had got the job: 'That's Julie Walters. I used to live below her when we worked together at the Everyman Theatre in Liverpool.' In her real universe, as in the one she would create on television, it was indeed a small world.

Slowly but surely Wood's talents were beginning to be recognised. Director David Leland was so impressed with her contribution to *In At the Death* that he invited her to write a play for Sheffield's Crucible Theatre. Wood agreed to do it but also asked if she could perform her own act in the evenings. Leland agreed, enabling Wood to develop both her theatrical career and her comic skills.

The play staged in Sheffield was *Talent*. It was a musical, set mainly backstage at a talent competition in a northern club. Wood vigorously denied that the inspiration came from her experiences on *New Faces*. Her play showed the seedy end of the entertainment industry, the bottom rung where the casting couch ruled and people were prepared to do anything just to get that first break. The carpet on-stage was intentionally so grimy Wood had to leave a note for the cleaners to stop them from continually shampooing it. In the stage version a lecherous man indulged in two instances of breast-squeezing. By the time the play was screened on ITV in 1979, this had been cut down to one, but the tawdriness remained firmly intact.

Julie (played on TV by Julie Walters) was the aspiring Shirley Bassey-inspired chanteuse; Maureen played by Wood was her plump but more sensible chum who was more interested in Monopoly than sex. As the characters prepare for the show you can see Julie's life mapped out in front of her. She is dreaming of an escape into the showbiz dreamworld, but we all know that she is heading for dishwashers and domesticity, screaming kids and a scheming husband. She would always want to escape, but, like many of her council estate contemporaries, she would never quite make it. It was a script riddled with wit and pathos. 'I thought *coq au vin* was love in a lorry,' comments the defiantly unsophisticated Julie.

Maureen and Julie may have seemed like caricatures to some people in the south, but in the north of England they were tragicomically all too real. There is something in the northern sense of humour which is about making things seems worse than they really are, but things couldn't get much bleaker than this.

The irony was that Wood began to make a success out of portraying abject failure. *Talent* had already transferred to the ICA in London before being screened on television, where it received rave reviews. But if press coverage is to be believed, Wood was unaware that television had made her an overnight sensation for the second time. According to reports at the time, she was broke. She was living in her £13 a week garret drinking milk out of a bottle and eating biscuits. No one could call her: the phone was off the hook because she didn't want to be disturbed while she was working. She didn't see any reviews because she could not afford the newspapers. The first inkling she had was when reporters doorstepped her and asked her

OPPOSITE:

A rare night out with Geoffrey Durham, husband and magician.

ABOVE:

As her fame grew, Wood came out of her shell off-stage as well as on it.

what it felt like to be called 'a genius'. It all seemed too far-fetched – far more unrealistic than anything Wood could write. And not strictly true either. In reality, she was at home with Geoffrey Durham, and she was too *anxious* to read her reviews, but asking him to select the most favourable ones.

The success of *Talent* kicked off Wood's career as a playwright. Like Alan Bennett and John Godber, she would go on to portray the north of England in a light that was loving, never harsh. She might concentrate on women and often characterise men as inadequate and dithering, vulnerable and awkward, but she was no ball-breaking militant feminist with a political axe to grind. She just found many men funny; that was the way she saw them.

Her relationship with Geoffrey was an intriguing one. For four years they lived out of each other's pockets in their small flat in Oxford Street. During the daytime he would practice his magic. So that she didn't get disturbed by the frequent cries of '*Olé*', she would do her writing when he was asleep – midnight to six, in longhand at a desk by a window overlooking the bus depot.

Wood gave the press typically short shrift when they started to show an interest in their partnership. What was it like for a comic and a magician to live together, they wondered? The somewhat exaggerated response came as no surprise. 'He doesn't run around with flowers coming out of his sleeves and I don't run around the house telling hilarious one-liners. Most of the time we are stuck in gloom over the kitchen table.'

As they each developed their careers, they pooled their resources. Their work often overlapped in the early days. In some relationships like this there might have been a risk of the woman becoming the magician's assistant, but this partnership was too equal and Wood too talented for that. Instead, Durham taught her some magic tricks so that when they performed together there was plenty of material to go round. Eventually she could cut people's hands off with a Black and Decker as well as Durham could. It was almost as if Wood had two double acts in her life: one with Geoffrey Durham and one with Julie Walters.

The end of the 1970s found Victoria Wood on a roll. In the spring of 1980 she married Geoffrey Durham. Wood has confessed to being not very romantic, but this was taking 'coolness' into hitherto uncharted waters. The priceless sequence of events could have come straight out of one of Wood's plays. She claimed he had been asking her to marry him every day since they had met. When she finally relented they went to Morecambe Registry Office – to discover that it was licensed only to issue death certificates. Morecambe was, after all, the kind of place elderly folk would go to die in, not to plight their troth.

Instead, their wedding took place in nearby Lancaster with the minimum number of witnesses present. Afterwards, they retired to a nearby cafe for spaghetti on toast. It was 10.30 in the morning, and that was what they felt like eating. Unfortunately the wedding photos were later mislaid on a bus, so the great day remains largely undocumented. When Granada Television found out about the marriage they sent the happy couple beige matching towels. Wood changed them for pink ones.

Nineteen eighty was a significant year for Wood. As well as her marriage it was notable for the transmission of her second musical play, *Nearly a Happy Ending*. This marked another appearance for Wood as Maureen, the dowdy, wistful sidekick in *Talent*. This time Maureen wants a man and in her desperation to get one – any one – she is determined to lose weight. This involves regular trips to the local baths so that she can 'swim to slim'. In reality, this meant frequent trips to the pool for Wood too, who, reversing the dramatic commitment of Robert De Niro (who had recently piled on the pounds to play Jake La Motta in *Raging Bull*), had to shed three stone so that she could then be padded up at first and show the weight loss later. When Maureen finally reaches her target weight, she is ready for sex with Tony and wants to 'get on with it' with almost clinical enthusiasm: 'Oh, foreplay…you don't have to. We can always do it afterwards, if there's time.'

Wood had another play on at the Crucible in Sheffield in 1980. That it wasn't as great a success as *Talent* may have been something to do with the subject matter. *Good Fun* was about a local community arts centre's attempts to have a charity event to raise money for cystitis sufferers. It was full of the kind of lines you might overhear at a gynaecologist's clinic, yet on-stage they took on a surreal quality. One character for instance, had had an unwanted pregnancy: 'She had an IUD but it slipped due to her trampolining. She demonstrates magnetic window cleaners now.'

Despite giving her the wrong colour towels as a wedding present, Granada Television had developed a very healthy working relationship with Wood. After the success of her first two plays, they were keen for a third one. Wood was less enthusiastic. She didn't want to keep milking the same characters until they ran dry. It was better to leave the viewer wanting more of Maureen than for Maureen to outstay her welcome. So Wood proposed that instead of another play, she should have a sketch series. There was also one inevitable proviso – that her best friend Julie should be in it. On 1 January 1982, *Wood and Walters* made its network debut.

RIGHT:
Cosy jumpers
suggested that knitting's
loss was comedy's gain.

. . . .
'Oh, foreplay...
you don't have to.
We can always do it
afterwards, if
there's time'
. . . .

From Dole Queue to Theatrical Cue

3

As Seen On TV

When Wood and Walters *was screened on ITV on Sunday nights, Victoria Wood became a full-blown celebrity. Gone were the days when the streets would empty and the nation would sit down as one to watch* Hancock *or* Steptoe and Son, *but for an intelligent, articulate comedian with ideas as well as one-line gags, this was as good as it got.*

The press, of course, got the wrong end of the stick. The combination of the names Wood and Walters had such an attractive ring to it that the tabloids couldn't resist suggesting they were some kind of long-running double act. Immediately they were acclaimed as the female successors to Morecambe and Wise. Journalists conveniently forgot that Walters was a successful actress in her own right and that Wood had been slogging her way back to the top ever since she thought she had been handed success on a plate when she collected her £75 pay cheque from New Faces.

OPPOSITE:

In character for
Pat and Margaret
with Julie Walters.

It was all rather disconcerting, being a success, thought Wood. Aspiring comics wrote asking for advice and fan mail started to come through the door. As a young girl she had only ever penned a fan letter to writer Keith Waterhouse. She had written to Peter Ustinov and Willie Rushton asking for advice, but the former didn't have any and the latter didn't reply. When people asked her, she didn't have much advice either, except to say that they were 'raving mad'. But maybe a competitive quality also meant that she didn't particularly want to help out any potential opposition.

Despite the acclaim, she was still riddled with both shyness and self-doubt. There was the understandable insecurity that she might simply dry up and not be funny any more, but she also confessed to more irrational fears: 'I worry about having a baby in case it grows up and can't find a parking space. Or that I will wake up in the morning and find that my hair has been replaced by two dead lemmings and some Shredded Wheat.'

LEFT:
Grinning and bearing it: another publicity stunt.

The ITV series made people laugh and even, predating the imminent alternative comedy boom, attracted a certain amount of notoriety. This was the era of medical breakthroughs in the field of fertility. In 1978 the first 'Test Tube Baby' had been born and multiple births were becoming commonplace. In one sketch Wood played a young mum who had produced around 740 babies at one sitting: 'We think it was 742, but a couple got mislaid when we left the hospital.' Every aspect of parenthood was taken to an absurd conclusion. In a room surrounded by toddlers, the mum

. . . .

'I worry about having a baby in case it grows up and can't find a parking space. Or that I will wake up in the morning and find that my hair has been replaced by two dead lemmings and some Shredded Wheat'

. . . .

LEFT:
The overcoat – like her comedy it was another layer to protect Wood from the outside world.

ABOVE:
Receiving an award and the attention of veteran comic Norman Wisdom.

OPPOSITE:
The blazer and limp tie were her trade-mark show clothes for a while.

had given up trying to feed them. Instead she had pointed out the grill and fish-fingers and told them to get on with it. A labour was so long the doctor who delivered the first baby had retired by the end of it.

One viewer, however, was not impressed. She wrote and asked whether Victoria Wood would now be using blind and crippled people as the inspiration for her sketches. Wood replied: 'Thanks for the idea.'

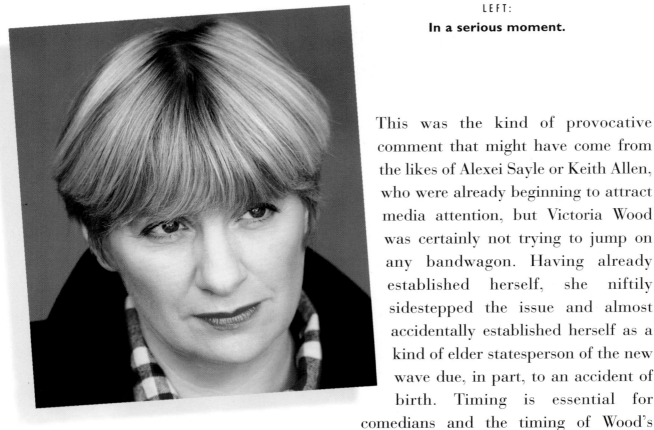

LEFT:
In a serious moment.

This was the kind of provocative comment that might have come from the likes of Alexei Sayle or Keith Allen, who were already beginning to attract media attention, but Victoria Wood was certainly not trying to jump on any bandwagon. Having already established herself, she niftily sidestepped the issue and almost accidentally established herself as a kind of elder statesperson of the new wave due, in part, to an accident of birth. Timing is essential for comedians and the timing of Wood's birth couldn't have been better. But it was a position she didn't necessarily embrace. When asked where she fitted in, she felt she was the last of the music hall turns, not part of the new wave: 'more in the tradition of people who sit around in freezing cold dressing rooms on wet Sunday afternoons waiting to go on'.

Around that time she cited her heroes as Max Miller, Joyce Grenfell and Tony Hancock. Even Hancock, now better known as a TV star, had cut his teeth in variety. Wood had loved Joyce Grenfell since that brief meeting in Buxton. As for Max Miller, the attraction was interesting. He was certainly ruder than Wood and a southerner, but in his flowery suits and cheeky manner there was a saucy, camp seaside-postcard appeal to his act which Wood's routines, with their women's waterworks problems and references to sex and underwear, also boasted.

She didn't feel famous though. That March she told *Cosmopolitan* that, 'Success belongs to other people, like imitation fur fabric pencil cases.' She confessed that her two awards to date were hardly taking pride of place in her Lancashire home (she had now moved with Geoffrey out of Morecambe to the village of Silverdale, where you could just see the sea if you balanced carefully on top of a counter). One was in a carrier bag with the Christmas decorations, while the other was behind a rubber plant with a string of plaster sausages on its head.

One of the fringe benefits of fame was the chance to film a lucrative ad in the Bahamas. It was for the popular diet drink of the day, One-Cal, which Wood said was 'for those who see the world through lettuce-coloured glasses'. It seemed a bit odd that someone overweight (albeit only slightly) was advertising a product to help people slim, and maybe Wood was self-conscious about this too. Just to show that she was not biased, she did an ad for chocolate the following year.

There was another handy spin-off to the TV fame. Wood and Geoffrey Durham's live show, *Funny Turns*, was also acclaimed – though a number of people must have turned up expecting to see the same sketches they had seen on Sunday nights 'on the box'. Instead, they had Wood at the piano and The Great Soprendo chopping up willing participants and shrieking *'Olé'*. *Funny Turns* was a huge success and soon transferred from the King's

'success belongs to other people, like imitation fur fabric pencil cases'

LEFT:
**The stylish comic turns
on the comic style.**

Head in Islington, the land of stripped pine and pot-pourri that Wood would find as inspiring as the north, to the Duchess Theatre in the West End of London.

As well as having a successful television career, Wood was now able to start building up the loyal live following which would be her bread and butter in the 1990s and help her to break records at the Royal Albert Hall. In October 1983 she returned to the King's Head with an all-new solo show, *Lucky Bag*.

In *Lucky Bag*, the piano and the songs were finally beginning to take more of a back seat. In their place Wood was developing a powerful stand-up act and a wide variety of characters. One new fictional creation was blue comic Paula Duval, who wore a black wig, a purple crimplene dress and carried a ukelele. She may have been inspired by some of Wood's own late-night gigs. She once admitted that one of her worst experiences was when she was booked under the misguided impression that she was a blue comic.

In another routine Wood played a poncho-wearing guide who was taking a party of tourists around the Brontës' parsonage in Haworth. After speculating on the poor health of the sisters and the lack of perms in 19th-century Yorkshire ('Charlotte would probably not be dead if she were alive today'), she encouraged the tourists to partake of Brontëburgers at the Heathcliff nosher bar. For anyone who dares to suggest that Wood was not a political comic, there was a cheap gag at the expense of Branwell Brontë: 'He was lazy, conceited and a dipsomaniac, so these days he'd have probably been in the government.' Hardly satire worthy of Swift but still very funny.

In another sketch she played a plucky posh-school monitor who was arguing at the debating society in favour of school uniforms. If families could not afford uniforms, she blamed the fathers for not passing their accountancy exams. She also argued that people would not know she was the Punishment Monitor if she were not allowed to wear her red Punishment Tie. Finally, she pointed out that her father was the sole supplier of uniforms for the school and that anyone who voted for her would get a discount.

As for Wood's own on-stage uniform, she had developed her own distinctly sloppy style which could roughly be described as cuddly new waver: a ubiquitous patterned jacket, shirt and tie, but the tie had to be at half-mast, like some long lost descendent of a St Trinian's.

By 1984 Wood was firmly in the comedy mainstream, though she was still considered young enough, and thus alternative enough, for the fledgling Channel 4 to repeat her ITV sketch-series. It was a strange position, straddling old and young comedy generations, but one which helped Wood to consolidate her position. But there was a strong sense that it was time to move on. Her original mentor at Granada, producer Peter Eckersley, had died just as *Wood and Walters* started; and despite the series' success, it seemed that Wood, forever the perfectionist, was never 100 per cent satisfied with it. Eckersley had been an integral cog in her transfer to television and he was no longer there to guide her. It was time for a move to the BBC.

Unfortunately not everything was running smoothly for Wood. There was talk of a film, *The Natural Order*, about the sexual relationship between a teacher and a pupil, which didn't

LEFT:
Bridging the gap between the mainstream and the alternative comedy world.

materialise. And then there were problems at the BBC. A new tour was planned to coincide with her new series. To capitalise on her imminent TV fame, her posters had the words 'Victoria Wood – As Seen On TV' printed across them. Unfortunately, 'due to circumstances beyond her control', a phrase that continuity announcer Susie Blake would make regular use of when the series was finally screened, the transmission of Wood's BBC debut was delayed, and the tour was badly attended. 'There were nights when I was glad to be overweight because it meant I could surround the audience,' joked Wood. 'Touring the Wood way' was a decidedly civilised affair, complete with orange juice and tea-bags. John Dowie's good behaviour had left its mark on her – there were no Keith Moon-style TV-defenestrating antics here: 'A couple of dry sherries and that's about it', she confessed to the Sunday Times. Still, some good came out of the timing – she derived the title of her new TV show out from scheduling fiasco.

'If her bum were a bungalow she'd never get a mortgage on it'

In January 1985 *Victoria Wood As Seen On TV* finally made it on to BBC2. Wood's world of varicose veins, crimplene, discontinued lines and brand-name biscuits won over more fans. The star and writer would become more popular than ever, but still didn't think she was a 'proper' star. With her homely personality, Lancashire accent, large eyes and 'funny' looks she felt she was an odd kind of celebrity. As she told Maureen Paton in the *Daily Express*: 'I could never see myself in a posh evening gown in the back of a limo... I'll have a good wash but that's about my limit.' Besides, being a TV personality didn't solve all of your problems at a stroke: 'It doesn't stop your fan belt from snapping.'

As Seen On TV marked the fully-fledged establishment of Wood's repertory company: Celia Imrie, Susie Blake, token male Duncan Preston and, of course, Julie Walters. Although Wood and Walters were no longer seen as a double act, there was never any question that they would stop working together. As Wood told the *Daily Express* in September 1986: 'I can see our partnership going on forever. We will be old ladies in wheelchairs, still making jokes about sex.'

OPPOSITE:
Wood's roots might have been in performance, but she also wanted to express the more thoughtful side of her character.

There was an intriguing temporary addition to the line-up, too. The actress Patricia Routledge had previously been noticed by the public after her stage appearance in Alan Bennett's *A Woman Of No Importance* in 1982. She appeared in *As Seen On TV* as Kitty, a Mancunian woman of a certain age who appeared to be a lady of leisure but who would make things with a sewing machine if the mood took her. Kitty's malapropish monologues addressed issues of the day, but from a strange, post-menopausal angle. Kitty, unlike most of Wood's creations – but very like Hyacinth Bucket, the character Routledge would later play in the sitcom, *Keeping Up Appearances* – was utterly middle class. In fact thirty years earlier she could have been played by Wood's great heroine, Joyce Grenfell. Kitty did have some strange habits. In one monologue she set out the demands that she had put to the BBC when they had asked her to work for them. She asked for a driver who had no blemishes – not on his driving licence, nor on his face: 'I'm not coming all the way from Cheadle glued to somebody's carbuncles.'

Routledge was just one of the ways in which Bennett and Wood would be linked. After Kitty, Patricia Routledge went back to work with Bennett on his BBC series of monologues, *Talking Heads*, portraying a highly disturbed yet terribly middle-class woman in *A Lady Of Letters*. Julie Walters starred in *Her Big Chance*, another programme in Bennett's series, in which she played an aspiring actress forever destined to be on the fringes, who wasn't a million miles away from Julie in *Talent*.

Other classic characters in *As Seen On TV* included Susie Blake's snobbish southern continuity announcer. She once appeared on the screen in the middle of the programme to apologise to northern viewers not, as you might expect, because there was transmission interference on the channel but simply because they had to live in the north.

LEFT:
The BBC series pushed Wood's profile to greater heights.

OPPOSITE:
Julie Walters: small eyes, big personality.

Wood and Walters continued working as a double act when the sketches required it. One of the best routines involved them playing aimless teenagers, Kelly-Marie and her pal, who would hang about on street corners, chewing bubble gum and talking about everything from boyfriends to drinking battery acid. Lines of sardonic dialogue reminiscent of the music hall star Norman Evans's over-the-wall gossips peppered these sketches: 'If her bum were a bungalow she'd never get a mortgage on it.'

Then, of course, there was Chrissie, a pathos-fuelled teenage long-distance swimmer played by Wood covered in goose grease. Chrissie was about to swim the English Channel, but her parents didn't seem to care. They were in London watching an Andrew Lloyd Webber musical while she braved the elements.

Wood and Walters also regularly teamed up as Joan and Margery, two TV presenters with something of an 'attitude' problem and a distinct lack of chemistry.

RIGHT:
Thoughtful: the grown-up Victoria Wood dresses down again.

'I could never see myself in a posh evening gown in the back of a limo... I'll have a good wash but that's about my limit'

Whenever they cropped up, interviewing a Houdini 'wannabe', for instance, or talking about cake decorations, you knew it was going to end in tears.

It was another recurring sketch, however, that captured public imagination. The best way of describing *Acorn Antiques* is to print the opening stage directions as they appeared in the book of Wood's work, *Chunky* (Methuen): 'Scene One. A tiny set, very artificial looking. An antique shop. Through the back door is a kitchen, with the end of a draining board and then a gap where the flattage has run out. Outside the shop window is a crooked photo of the street. All the actors in this serial are over made-up (women) or speak ironically (men). Babs is blonde, sitting by a blank wall-plan. She's on the phone, holding it well away from her face for the camera. Music.'

What this doesn't capture, however, is the sheer unadulterated mayhem of the spoof soap, or the closing credits, which were mounted on transparent cards but never appeared quite as level as they should have been. Against stiff competition from Celia Imrie (Babs), Duncan Preston (Clifford) and Wood (Bertha), it was Julie Walters who did the upstaging and took the overacting honours as Mrs Overall, the cleaning lady who couldn't hit a cue if it was staring her in the face. Her lines overlapped, camera angles were blocked; this strange creature, who bore a striking resemblance to the commode-pusher Victoria Wood had met at Manchester Poly in 1970, walked away with the show.

Inevitably people compared the rank amateurism of *Acorn Antiques* to *Crossroads*, the Midlands motel soap which, at the time, was still running. Mrs Overall also bore a stunning resemblance to Amy Turtle, the ageing, line-forgetting dogsbody of the motel. Surprisingly, Wood denied that it was the main influence. Maybe she feared litigation. Instead she compared the wobbly-walled send-up to the day-time soaps, which made the production values of *Crossroads* seem extravagant. Interestingly, *Crossroads* was axed soon after *Acorn Antiques* appeared. Could the makers have been shamed by the similarity?

Victoria Wood As Seen On TV was a hysteria-inducing combination of Beryl Cook's bawdiness, Alan Bennett's linguistic nuances and Pinteresque absurdity – not to mention Eccles cakes, ovaries, Hobnobs, Vimto and Gypsy Creams. No wonder it scooped a BAFTA. More surprisingly it didn't pick up a commendation from biscuit manufacturers McVities.

Suddenly writing and performing seemed to take up every moment for Victoria Wood. At one point she worked every day for four months. She had to write a play, sixty sketches for television and eight songs. Her diary, once filled with little more than lighting-up times, was now jammed. It was as if she was making up for lost time in the post-*New Faces* dole-queue phase.

4

'My Other Hat's A Balaclava'

Success can bring awards, money and increased popularity. It does not automatically confer supreme confidence on the recipient even if onlookers think it does. By 1986, with two series of As Seen On TV under her belt, Victoria Wood was arguably the funniest television personality in the country. She would not like gender to be brought into the debate, but she was certainly the funniest female television personality. Yet she could still come out with lines that suggested that her ego was more fragile than the scenery in Acorn Antiques. That November she told the Daily Mirror that 'Some mornings I sit up in bed convinced my brain has fallen out in the night and I've lost it somewhere under the pillow.' It was obviously a joke couched in terms of self-deprecation, but that certainly didn't mean that she didn't feel that way about her abilities.

OPPOSITE:
**If the cap fits: receiving
one of her many
honorary degrees.**

Perhaps it was no surprise she had an identity crisis. However successful she was, she seemed to be mistaken for somebody else. In the early days it was poet Pam Ayres. Then it was Dawn French. The two comics would become friends and there would be room for both of them in the comic firmament, but that didn't mean that Wood didn't sense some competition coming along. Many of the people she admitted to liking around this time, such as playwrights Noel Coward and Joe Orton were far too dead to be seen as serious contemporary rivals.

In 1987 the public were eager for another television series, but instead Wood went on the road again. Hands shoved into her pockets, sleeves rolled up, she would regale an audience with tales of housecoats and Bovril, occasionally slinking back to the piano stool for a song. Apart from Dave Allen, she was virtually the only stand-up comic to do some of her act sitting down. By now she was a vegetarian, supplementing her diet with vitamins, but this wasn't an early attempt at political correctness. She had no ideological problems with wearing shoes made from animal skins or with leather handbags. In fact the whole advent of PC was complex for a comedy *aficionado* of Wood's generation. She was certainly not racist, but she admitted in the *Independent* that while she found fellow comedian Bernard Manning's attitudes hateful, he could still make her laugh. By the time her show reached the London Palladium in October it was a fine-tuned mixture of character comedy and straight stand-up, with a few obligatory songs thrown in. Wood took on the persona of a desperate, self-deluded make-up artist attempting to get people to sample the 'new look'; she would play an anonymous middle-aged lady blundering into the stalls. She was no Bernard Manning, but she had her cruel moments. Apologising for her colourful coat, she pointed out that the person who had made it was colour-blind. She sang the praises of the nearby snack-bar Spud-U-Like: 'Like the DSS with potatoes.' For anyone who thought Wood was becoming cosy, she proved she had a dangerous streak – a strictly suburban dangerous streak. She dreamt of running into Laura Ashley and shouting 'polyester', or untidying the jumper piles in Benneton.

So was Victoria Wood becoming a part of the establishment? It certainly seemed to be the case when on 1 October 1988 she gave birth to baby daughter Grace at the Portland Hospital – two months after the Duchess of York had given birth there. 'I knew it was the VIP suite,' Wood joked to *Woman*. 'I found a couple of long ginger hairs under the pillow.'

She was obviously ready to become a mother. She said, 'I've studied the symptoms of pregnancy: moody, big bosoms, irritable. I've obviously been pregnant for twenty years.' Wood denied that

OPPOSITE:
At the Palladium: notice her hero Max Miller on the bill above.

ABOVE:
With Emma Thompson, whose brief forays into comedy couldn't compete with Wood's sustained wit.

the choice of the Portland was a sign of snobbery; she just wanted the privacy that she wouldn't have got in her local hospital. Besides, even if it was snobbery, she undercut it by travelling there from her Maida Vale flat on the London Underground. She also undercut any sense of elitism and maternal empowerment by suggesting that the surgeon decided to induce the baby on a Friday because he had a golf match on the Saturday.

She had decided to keep silent about the pregnancy to avoid it becoming a media circus. In the summer she had been six months' pregnant when she filmed *An Audience With Victoria Wood* for LWT, which picked up two BAFTA Awards, but thanks to a baggy top none of the journalists spotted the new bulge.

One might have thought that the birth of a child would have meant a career being put on to the back burner. In fact the way Grace was conceived and born suggests that Wood had planned her entrance into motherhood with the strategy of a military tactician. She wanted to conceive at the beginning of the year so that the early months of the pregnancy wouldn't clash with any professional engagements. To achieve this she said she had flown back to Heathrow from a booking in Dublin to be with Geoffrey Durham. It may have sounded clinical but it did the trick and nine months later Grace was born, with the aid of an epidural and the Olympics synchronised swimming on the television. Once again Wood was fairly dispassionate about the process. She couldn't see the attraction of natural childbirth, remarking that 'when you break a leg you don't say to the doctor, "don't give me an anaesthetic,

'I've studied the symptoms of pregnancy: moody, big bosoms, irritable. I've obviously been pregnant for twenty years.'

LEFT:
Shopping for the children — even celebrities have to visit Mothercare.

61

. . . .
'I found a couple of long ginger hairs under the pillow'
. . . .

I want to feel the pain.""' In one of those moments that could have come out of her sketches about nice middle-class Islington couples whose lives are dominated by fireguards and sea-sponge tampons, the placenta was dropped and Wood complained to the nurse that she had wanted to eat it. It was obviously a joke, what with Wood being vegetarian.

As it happens, Wood actually would be unlikely to incorporate this incident into her act. She has made it very clear that the Victoria Wood on-stage is a persona. Although they surely aren't a million miles apart, she has a very clear dividing line between her real life and her stage life. Similarly, she has never made jokes about her parents or her siblings.

In fact, despite popular opinion and the fact that she is a self-confessed eavesdropper, she claims not to use overheard conversations as dialogue. She

LEFT:
Henry Durham goes walkies; Wood took motherhood in her stride, quickly returning to work, pausing only to breast-feed.

once recalled how she had been at a rather up-market dinner party. She was sitting quietly, basically because she was so shy, when a woman turned and remarked, 'Look at her, drinking it all in.' Nothing could have been further from the truth.

Motherhood seemed to suit her. She soon went back to her writing, but not before declaring that her daughter came first: 'I'm not happy unless I've wiped her bottom every day.' When Grace was a few months old, Wood set out on another national tour. It was her life-blood as well as financially rewarding: 'Stage is my real job, television is how I reach a wider audience. You can't beat performing in front of a live audience, there just isn't the same excitement in front of the cameras.'

. . . .

'Stage is my real job, television is how I reach a wider audience. You can't beat performing in front of a live audience, there just isn't the same excitement in front of the cameras'

. . . .

ABOVE:
Happiness is performing live: Wood relaxing.

By 1989, however, she was back in front of the cameras, in various new guises. Victoria Wood had been true to her earlier words that she wanted to move on and had abandoned sketch comedy in favour of six eponymously titled thirty-minute playlets for BBC1 – she called them 'playdolinos'. They certainly weren't sitcoms, because, despite the running time, they were shot on film without a live audience and, most importantly, didn't have enough sofas. It was a big moment for her, transferring from the minority channel BBC2 to the mainstream channel. She may have started out on the mainstream commercial network with *Talent*, but although an established prime-time performer, she had never before had such a high-profile series. Julie Walters certainly thought she deserved the breakthrough. She said that 'Victoria is the funniest person in the world. I've never met anyone with such wit.'

The plays attacked both familiar targets and some new ones. In typically post-modern fashion, Wood had been developing a keen interest in the absurdity of television, particularly the low-budget end. It is something she has continued to do to this day. She had already addressed the issue with *Acorn Antiques* and *Joan and Margery*, and now her gaze was firmly fixed on daytime TV. Having been at

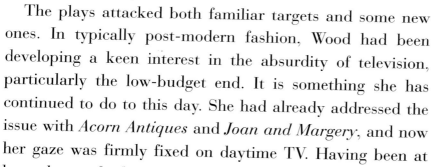

'I'll know that I'm really important when they let me in the car park'

home breast-feeding, she had joked that the television was the only thing that she saw apart from her own bosoms. Now *Over To Pam* was to be her fiercest assault on the housewives' opium. Wood's opinion was clear. She wondered if, instead of daytime television, the TV should just be a blank screen apart from a caption saying 'We have no television worth showing.'

In *Over To Pam*, Wood played a character called, 'Victoria Wood', who was accompanying hairdresser Lorraine, who was to be interviewed on *Live With Pam*, part of a brainless schedule that included *Chuck A Sausage* and *Take My Pet*. Victoria was an old hand at TV, she said; she had worked with Judith Chalmers before the latter was brown. It wasn't quite clear how much 'Victoria Wood' was supposed to be herself, but the script wasn't without its self-referential digs. In one scene, the Sloane Ranger researcher Caroline says how much she loves the 'dancing

'Professional northerners live in Barnes'

round the handbags' thing that Wood does, when actually she is thinking of French and Saunders. Wood joked about the rivalry between herself and the new comic duo, but there may well have been a grain of truth behind the gags. In an interview in *Time Out*, she said that she was working on a film script, but would say no more because 'Dawn and Jennifer would write it.'

As the backstage preparations for *Live With Pam* continue, it soon becomes clear that Pam (played with bitch-goddess authority by Julie Walters) wants to exploit Lorraine, dressing her in a tarty frock and painting a sob story of an Essex Girl who was a teenage mum and Valium addict who was sexually harrassed at work. In the end Pam doesn't go on the show, so Victoria dons a blonde wig and lurex bimbo dress and takes her place, shaming Pam for patronising her live on air so much that her contract is immediately cancelled. A distant relation of Pam, would, however, return to the Wood repertoire in the next decade in the play *Pat and Margaret*.

In the five other short plays Wood addressed more scenarios ripe for comedy. in *Val De Ree* she and Celia Imrie go hill-walking, getting soaked and falling out in the process; In *Mens Sana In Thingummy Doodah*, Wood, Walters and the team find themselves working out at a health farm, The Pinkney Hydro – 'Your Gateway To Health'. At least Victoria is there to work out, Walters played Nicola, the instructor who has a wind problem if she eats broccoli and turns out not to practise what she preaches. There were echoes of the earlier *Nearly A Happy Ending* in the character of Lil who was determined to lose weight under the impression that her boyfriend would then leave his wife for her. It is a comedy tinged with sadness. Even if she shed the requisite pounds, it is abundantly clear that he will never divorce his spouse.

Staying In was Victoria Wood's take on the middle-class dinner party circuit. It was a subject acutely dissected in Mike Leigh's *Abigail's Party*, but Wood handled things differently. There is no one here quite as monstrous as Beverly, Leigh's horrifying creation for Alison Steadman though Patricia Hodge's hostess Moira came close. Wood preferred a subtle drip-drip-drip of painful conversation rather than a sausage-on-a-stick, a heart attack and a nervous breakdown. Wood's real life, in which she didn't socialise a great deal, did, despite her denials, find itself reflected in her attitudes here: 'There isn't a cocktail party in the world that can compete with a baked potato and the *Antiques Roadshow*.'

The final two plays were *The Library* and *We'd Quite Like To Apologise*. They both, in their own ways, focus on the embarrassment of being English in a public situation. The first is a

OPPOSITE:
Wood and Grace in north London.

ABOVE:
**Another
northern bard –
Alan Ayckbourn.**

love story involving a repressed, awkward librarian; the second, despite a title that sounds like a line from Susie Blake's continuity announcer, is set at an airport where a flight is delayed. Again these are situations that other playwrights such as Leigh, John Godber or Alan Ayckbourn might look at: comedies of manners populated by little people leading little lives but drawn with broad strokes and supremely deft dialogue. The comparison with Mike Leigh is the most complex. Whereas he might be accused of patronising the working classes in his dramas, Wood seemed to understand and empathise with her subjects, even though she herself is every bit as middle class as Leigh. You only dislike people for the way they behave, not for an accident of birth.

The series was reasonably well received, but it was not the resounding success that her previous TV work had been. There were various explanations for this, but the answer is very simple and relates to the reason why Wood continues to be such a phenomenal live attraction. The series was made on film and not shot in front of a live audience. Although it was shown to a live audience before screening so that there was laughter on it, it fell

OPPOSITE:
**Promoting the
scripts of her BBC
'playdolinos'.**

between two televisual stools; it was neither a comedy-drama without an audience, like the *Comic Strip* films, nor a sitcom, where the cast feeds off the audience response. Wood had said live work was her life-blood; this, even more than her usual television work, was the complete antithesis. On the other hand, these shorts do show where her ideas were coming from and where they were going. The cruelty and sheer farce of *Over To Pam*, in particular, acts as a creative bridge between *Acorn Antiques* and the later, darker *Pat and Margaret*. The criticism did sting though. Perhaps that was why she remarked that 'I always wanted to be famous, but I didn't have much idea as what. I should have robbed a bank. It would have been a lot quicker than all this farting about writing scripts.'

Finally, 1989 was a year in which Wood drew appreciation from all directions. She finally seemed to have made it to the top on her own terms. There was talk of her starring in a film adaptation of the Jill Tweedie book, *Internal Affairs*, about a social worker from Kentish Town who becomes embroiled in a family planning fiasco in the Far East. The co-star was due to be Paul Hogan, then riding high on the back of *Crocodile Dundee*, but it was one of those hyped-up projects that sound intriguing but come to nothing.

Then there was the corporate entertainment booking to beat all corporate entertainment bookings. Wood flew to Nassau in the Bahamas for two days to entertain the great and the good of Derby boiler firm Gloworm. The thirty-minute show was reported to have cost Gloworm in the region of £22,000, but a spokesman said that Wood was worth every penny. This was a long way from other less successful private functions: in front of 400 drunk businessmen at midnight when she had followed a blue comedian and 'at a marquee in the afternoon with the sunlight glinting off your sweat.'

The year closed with a more prestigious, if less lucrative, honour. Wood became a Doctor of Letters at Lancaster University. She may have failed to get into Manchester Polytechnic, but the local comic seemed to have finally made it on home turf. In the light of the mixed reviews for her BBC series, she was less sure about whether she had been accepted at London's Television Centre: 'I'll know that I'm really important when they let me into the car park.'

Perhaps not surprisingly, given the harsh response of the critics, by 1990 Victoria Wood was talking about leaving television behind. In particular, she wanted to move even further away from sketch-comedy. At one point it seemed that she even wanted to move away from stand-up when she said that 'Jokes are harder than plays because they have to hit the nail on the head, a near miss is no good.' Then again, she wanted to embrace the challenge of long-form work. It was a way of developing substantial

BELOW:
**Wood looking up –
but in the late '70s
her name was yet
to be in lights.**

'Jokes are harder than plays because they have to hit the nail on the head, a near miss is no good'

LEFT:
The loosened tie and blazer – it could only be a stock-market trader or Victoria Wood.

OPPOSITE:
Noël Coward: the impeccable wordsmith was another role model Wood aspired to.

ideas, rather than just running through an unconnected shopping list of gags. Yet at times she felt that even her playlets now seemed too constricting as a creative vehicle.

Ultimately Wood appeared to want to go in opposite directions – towards longer, feature-length pieces, while at the same time continuing with her live stand-up work and those classic one-liners. She just wanted people to find her work funny. As she told *Time Out*: 'To be able to make people laugh is the nicest thing you can do for somebody really... apart from a blow-job or something.'

In 1990 live stand-up took precedence over television for Wood. She had been on tour since May and reached the Strand Theatre in September. It had been a demanding, punishing schedule, not least because she had taken Grace with her. Whenever Wood arrived at a hotel, the same ritual would take place: the breakables were moved out of reach, along with the pot-pourri and the alcohol from the mini-bar. Then it was safe to put Grace to bed. Some nights, of course, she wouldn't go to sleep. At one point she had chickenpox, and Wood took her down to the bar for the evening, wrapped in a blanket and disguised as a handbag.

The shows in the capital were less problematic. Victoria and Geoffrey had their flat in north London, and if he wasn't working Grace and Geoffrey could spend the evening at home together. The couple were still determined to retain their base in Lancashire. As she told the *Daily Express*: 'Professional northerners live in Barnes.'

The West End shows might have shocked fans who knew Wood from television. Apart from the woman from bedspread-makers Candlewick who allegedly

. . . .

'To be able to make people laugh is the nicest thing you can do for someone really... apart from a blow-job or something'

. . . .

complained about the scathing remarks about her quilts, most of her critics focused on the frank discussions about sex, much of it concentrating on the very suburban pastime of wife-swapping. Wood was typically self-effacing about the scale of the tour, describing her entourage as 'one manic depressive and an ironing board'. She thought she got a standing ovation, 'But maybe the audience was getting up to put its coat on.' The record-breaking run was a long way from an early gig which Wood later recalled. There had only been three people there, she could have given them all a lift home in her Mini.

On-stage at the Strand, Wood also broached the subject of faked orgasms. She claimed she had responded to a survey to measure her sex appeal. When she had sent her answers in, she received a reply reminiscent of the critical response from Bob Mason when she adjusted his flares: 'Very poor work – see me.'

Elsewhere, she offered new insights into the strange ways of the British – the only nation that could have invented the stationary caravan. Reviews were generally favourable, even though Milton Schulman in the *Evening Standard* got into rather a lather over the sexual content, not taking kindly to talk of ovulation and pregnancy-testing kits requiring women to pee on a paddle to find out if they had conceived.

It was no surprise that a man, rather than a woman, voiced his discomfort about the material... he had probably never been in a room where a group of women have had a few drinks and start talking among themselves – but it did put the issue of Wood's attitude to sex on the agenda. It was, and remains, a strange one. It would be all too easy to say her attitude is very English, very 'seaside postcard'. But hers is not necessarily a world where men are randy and big-busted women are 'begging for it'. For every suburban swinger who wanted to be bent over backwards on the hostess trolley, as Wood sang of Frieda, who couldn't quite persuade Barry to tear himself away from a vinyl floor covering catalogue, there was another who would rather have had a Horlicks than a spot of bedroom gymnastics. Her fans didn't seem that sexually motivated either. She said they were more interested in Mrs Overall than her underwear. Wood herself wouldn't be pressed on the subject, but in real life the woman once voted the person British people would most like as their next-door-neighbour, ahead of the Queen Mother, revealed that she would rather have a herbal peppermint tea than Typhoo and a Gypsy Cream. There was clearly a dividing line between Victoria Wood off and on-stage.

Magic Moments

N ot everything Victoria Wood touched turned to gold. In the spring of 1991 she recorded a track for the ubiquitous Comic Relief Appeal. She helped to make a comedy record that would raise money for charity but make music critics hang their heads in shame. Perhaps it was lucky for Wood that most of the media attention was focused on the flip-side, 'Stonk', by Hale and Pace. Her effort, the painful 'The Smile Song', found her trussed up in leather in the video, spoofing Kylie Minogue, Janet Jackson and the Pet Shop Boys. More promisingly, she was working on a film script, called Sisters, which would turn, after various trials and tribulations, into Pat and Margaret.

LEFT:
As the '90s took shape, Wood was looking for new challenges.

OPPOSITE:
Longer hair, looser clothes – an altogether more relaxed Victoria.

In May 1992, however, there was another success. Baby number two was born, once again at the Portland Hospital. With a name like Henry Wood, it was maybe fate that his mum's future live triumphs would be at the Royal Albert Hall. Another Henry Wood had founded the Promenade Concerts there nearly a century earlier. That might have made great copy, but, of course, this Henry's surname was Durham.

> **'A sandwich: take two bits of bread. Put them together. Now eat it.'**

After Henry's birth, Victoria Wood took a big step. The person who had, only a couple of years earlier, said that professional northerners live in Barnes, moved south. Not quite as far as Barnes but to Highgate in north London. It could hardly have been called 'selling out'. With so much of her work going on in the capital, it seemed absurd to be heading up and down the M6 each week – 'taking six hours to get to a meeting'. Besides, she decided, children of a famous person growing up in a small village would always attract attention. In a big city, particularly in an area full of people in the arts and the media, they would have more chance of melting into the background. Grace, for instance, soon started school alongside the offspring of actor Jonathan Pryce.

After spending so much time on the road, the second child and the subsequent time spent at home must have reminded Victoria Wood of the sheer awfulness of daytime television, because in the autumn of 1992 it was announced that she would be presenting the coveted BBC1 comedy spot on Christmas Day, fronting a show which sent up morning programming. It was the slot that was traditionally filled by Morecambe and Wise and further proof that Wood was up there with the comedy greats. The show was titled *The All-Day Breakfast* and was intended to be a send-up of early morning television, a period Wood described as 'all social conscience and ovaries'.

In *The All-Day Breakfast*, Wood teamed up with Duncan Preston to play a fictional version of Richard Madeley and Judy Finnegan. She was Sally Cumbernauld, he was Martin Crossthwaite; different surnames, but of course they were married.

Elsewhere the programme was ready to hit other TV targets. There was a spoof of the short-lived BBC soap *El Dorado*, in which Wood played Pam, a pink-hued imitation of ageing club crooner Trish Valentine, in a blonde wig with velvet trousers and gold stiletto slippers: 'I don't sing but I'm a very down to earth, brassy lady with a heart of gold who wears flirty blouses,' she explained.

OPPOSITE:

A rare public appearance with Henry.

ABOVE:
Wood rabbits with Warren: Victoria meets the man who was Alf Garnett – Warren Mitchell.

By 1993 Wood's life was falling neatly into place. She was still working as hard as ever, but things were better organised now. She had even shed a substantial amount of weight after years of being known euphemistically as a 'cuddly' comic. It transpired that she had an allergy to sugar. She cut it out of her diet and, perhaps not surprisingly, the pounds fell off. An almost obsessive interest in fitness videos helped too. The woman who seem to personify an anti-fitness lifestyle of cream puffs and milky tea had become a worshipper of Jane Fonda's workouts. It was a strange turnaround, but given the workload she was about to undertake it was also sensible.

. . . .
'My nose has grown so big, the rest of my face is applying for a council flat.'
. . . .

RIGHT:

Despite the self-deprecation, Wood's looks seemed to improve with age.

In April 1993 Wood set out on a seven-month tour that would culminate in her record-breaking fifteen nights at the Royal Albert Hall. She had to juggle parenthood with touring and did this by going away for four nights a week and being at home for three. Whenever possible she was driven back to Highgate after a gig, so that she was there for the children in the morning. She compared the punishing schedule to working on an oil rig. Fortunately the money was rather better.

Once again the London shows received their mixture of critical brickbats and bouquets, but the fans went wild. For every critic who pointed out that Wood had done the gag about the dyslexic lover who spent twenty minutes looking for the vinegar there were ten fans backstage waiting for a peak at their hero. Some, disturbingly, were even modelling themselves on Wood's characters. There were the *Acorn Antiques* fans, keen to show Wood the scripts they had written themselves following the spoof series (some even went as far as making a video). And then there were clones of Wood's female nerd in the yellow plastic beret-cum-rain hat, the one forever waiting for her friend Kimberly. We have never actually met Kimberly, but would recognise her here; she's the one who went to the boutique and bought the only thing that would fit her – the cubicle.

The shows did reveal a changed Victoria Wood, and not just physically. This was a comedian who now seemed more at ease with herself than ever. There were still the ego-puncturing asides – 'My nose has grown so big the rest of my face is applying for a council flat' – but these acted as a valve to release the pressure of being such a huge celebrity. She was able to laugh at her inadequacies in a way that only a female comedian could. By and large, male comedians would go on the offensive rather than admit to being less than perfect. This may have been the reason that when the alternative comics came to the fore, in comparison Wood was seen as not very threatening. But hers was a subtle, liberating, slow-burn aggression. Off-hand remarks might get a quick laugh, but later they would get an audience, particularly a female audience, thinking. Take her dinner party advice: 'Throw a brick through the dining room window to distract guests if the food is bad. Then serve up sandwiches while waiting for the police to arrive.' What better way could there be to defuse the stress and anxiety brought on by all that entertaining of husbands' bosses. Wood herself was not, it

. . . .

'If you go out listening you don't hear anything.'

. . . .

RIGHT:

An aggressive look, but Wood's material packed a more subtle punch.

seems, a great cook. She once supplied a charity cook book with the following recipe: 'A sandwich: take two bits of bread. Put them together. Now eat it.'

It is one of the complex aspects of Wood's sense of humour that two of its key elements are the result of an accident of birth; namely accent and sex. Living in London hasn't changed the first and it would take drastic action to change the second. There is no doubt that having a northern lilt lends a real humour to words that in another dialect would sound mundane. 'Chiropodist', 'poncho' or 'macaroons' suddenly take on a life of their own when uttered by Wood.

American playwright Neil Simon has suggested that this is because consonants are funnier than vowels, and it certainly seems to be the case with accents with a northern tinge to them. The same could be said of the way that Alan Bennett finds humour in simple, everyday words. The same could be said more recently of Mrs Merton, another product of Manchester or Reeves and Mortimer, whose verbal games add a surreal twist to their north-eastern accent. Wood has herself equated her lilting delivery to singing: 'It's very musical. It's all to do with rhythm and punctuation and building up an expected pattern and then breaking it and catching people on the off-beat.'

Some theorists might suggest that the dominance of northern humour has something to do with the fact that in the north people are more conversational; that wherever you go beyond Birmingham, there are innocent conversations taking place with a rich comic twang to them. Wood goes along with this theory up to a point, recalling how once she was in a coastal town where she overheard one woman telling another that the pier had burnt down. Wood expected the other to be sympathetic, to say how sorry she was. Instead she just answered with a brusque, 'About time, too.' Then again, although Wood liked nothing better than getting a crossed telephone line, she insisted she didn't go out of her way to appropriate comments: 'If you go out listening you don't hear anything.'

RIGHT:
Her asexual look attracted a strong gay following without alienating that crucial heterosexual fanbase.

'I was never really anti-men, but because there weren't too many women stand-ups around they assumed you were either a lesbian or a communist.'

Wood's other accidental asset was being born a woman. She would regularly be asked about the issue of 'women in comedy' but fought shy of entering into the debate about why there were fewer funny women than funny men. She admired females as well as men – by the early '90s she said she was a fan of the gynaecologically obsessed Joan Rivers alongside Peter Sellers, Ken Dodd, Woody Allen, Tony Hancock and Billy Connolly, Steve Coogan's Alan Partridge and Harry Enfield – but ultimately she didn't want to draw a sexual dividing line. She got rather exasperated at the idea that because she was a female comedian, she must, in some way, be intrinsically 'anti-men'. This was a label that men, not women, put on her. She told the *Daily Mirror*: 'I was never really anti-men, but because there weren't too many women stand-ups around they assumed you were either a lesbian or a communist.' She felt that some quarters of the media thought she was only funny because she was a woman, but she felt that her sex was irrelevant. Besides, she added, there may be fewer women than men comedians but there are also fewer women plasterers. Then again, she did acknowledge that there was something basically different between a male comic and a female comic: 'Men tell jokes, women tell stories, because women communicate whereas men just trade information.'

By far the saddest blot on the landscape in 1993 was the death of Wood's father

RIGHT:
Another cuppa.

OPPOSITE:
With Duncan Preston, her regular leading man.

Stanley in November. Stanley was eighty-two and had only recently stopped working as an insurance salesman. Hard work and a refusal to give up clearly ran in the family. His death hit Wood hard; her way of coping seemed to be to bury herself in even more work. If 1993 had been an intensive year 1994 would top even that.

Victoria Wood hadn't had a full-length play put on since the early '80s. She had started work on various scripts and ideas – there was talk, for instance, of an autobiographical piece set in 1969 – but by the early '90s nothing had materialised. And then in 1991 word had got out that she was working on the aforementioned script, *Sisters*, about two long lost siblings being reunited.

By 1994 the screenplay was being filmed, but it had had a gestation far more painful than that of Wood and Durham's real children. Initally LWT had bought the script. They were very excited about it and planned to spend £6 million and give the project a cinematic release. With one of the fictional sisters having relocated to America and become a Joan Collins-type soap star, they saw huge transatlantic potential. And then, according to reports at the time, they didn't see huge transatlantic potential. According to Wood she awaited their comments on a draft but they didn't come. Suddenly, ITV felt it didn't have the commercial prospects they were initially so confident about. Wood was understandably livid, particularly as, she claimed, she had already spent the advance. Eventually, she calmed down and did raise the money to buy the rights back. She then sold them to the BBC for less, but at least she was fairly confident the project, now retitled *Pat and Margaret*, would be made, albeit for television's Screen One slot rather than the cinema.

When *Pat and Margaret* was finally transmitted on 11 September 1994, it was clear that ITV's loss was the BBC's gain. This was Wood's deepest, most layered work to date, at times cringe-makingly funny, at times undoubtedly cruel. It reminded viewers that Wood was a playwright who could spin out a considerable story and imbue it with a wicked Ortonesque viciousness, not just make gags about tacky television and Pot Noodles.

Then again, *Pat and Margaret* was actually inspired by television that, if not cheap, was certainly shallow. Wood had been watching programmes such as *Surprise Surprise*, where estranged relations were re-introduced on camera, and wondered what happened after the credits had finished rolling. Did the people go back to their very different lives? Was their relationship altered forever or did things return to what they had been before? Could they *ever* return to what they had been before?

In *Pat and Margaret* Victoria Wood played Margaret Mottershead, a dowdy cleaner with a dodgy perm. Julie Walters played Pat Bedford,

OPPOSITE:
A cheerful Wood: a smile for the press hid the fact that when the cameras were put away she took things more seriously.

the soap star now based in America. (The characters did have their antecedents: Wood had already used a Mottershead in one of her eponymous BBC playlets, while Pat bore more than a passing resemblance to Pam in *Over To Pam*).

While Pat was over in the UK promoting her book, the sisters were thrown together for the first time in twenty-seven years on the show *Magic Moments*. In front of the audience there was a great deal of emotion. Pat used it to show her human side, hugging her sister and shedding the odd tear. Backstage, she was ready to be whisked back to her hotel before her next engagement. Equally she expected Margaret to head straight back to her job as chip fryer at the all-day breakfast counter at Kirkby Preston motorway service station and life with illiterate Jim, a lavatory cleaner, and his mum, played with her usual northern charm by Thora Hird.

It was a brilliant, and utterly credible conceit, although with hindsight, maybe an illiterate, dyslexic lavatory cleaner was somewhat gilding the rather grim lily. But there was more here than met the eye. As Wood said of these real-life separations: 'There must be a good reason for not seeing these people all that time.'

Pat Bedford, as portrayed by Walters, is, at first, one of Wood's all-time classic monsters, although she later turns out to be more human than it first appears. She is the kind of celebrity who believes her own press releases and describes herself as 'an icon' (in an interview to promote the film, Wood told *The Times* 'I can't say my iconicity weighs heavily on me, though').

As it turned out, *Pat and Margaret* had more in common than they were initially prepared to admit. As Pat says, she 'came sixth in the World's Most Envied Bottom Poll in 1992. How can I be related to a woman whose buttocks practically skim the carpet?' They find, however, that they have a shared goal. When the tabloids set off to find their mother to get a scoop, the chase is on for them to uncover her first. And Wood slips in a neat twist there, too. Their mother is not some dotty old senior citizen, but a former prostitute who used to 'do it standing up for 10 Bensons, laying down for 20'.

Wood clearly found the story fascinating because it was about the way people try to divorce themselves from their pasts. It was a predicament in which she was increasingly finding herself, as she moved south and mixed with different people to those she had encountered in Ramsbottom. Furthermore, like Pat, Wood's identity crisis was compounded by the fact that she had an onscreen identity and a 'real' identity – she knew where one ended and the other began, even though her fans didn't.

Pat and Margaret tied together all sorts of themes in Wood's life and philosophy. It was also about how intrusive the press can be;

she had always kept her family out of her professional life as much as possible. The children had her husband's name and she said she never made jokes about them, him, her siblings or parents, although you can't help feeling that a gag about childbirth was based on her own experiences: 'Having a baby is a bit like watching two inefficient removal men trying to get a very large sofa through a very small door – and you can't tell them to send it round through the French windows.' Then again, Wood happily fictionalises her attitudes to get a laugh. She says she loves babies yet she also hatched the following gag: 'She said she had post-natal depression. Then she showed me the baby. Then I had it as well.'

'Just because I look cosy doesn't mean I am'

The currents of *Pat and Margaret* ran deeper than anything Wood had written before. It was also about the sensitive subject of how patronising southerners could be about northerners. And also about how celebrities could have an over-inflated sense of their own importance. Wood denied that Pat Bedford was based on Raquel Welch but told a story at the time of how she had been at a function with Welch and had been told, for reasons which were never made fully clear to her, that she mustn't stand too close to her. She also heard that Welch, allegedly, brought her own mirror with her to Britain.

Most of all, though, *Pat and Margaret* touched on the very nature of fame, how success breeds jealousy. At one point Margaret says to Pat: 'I want what you've got,' and Pat says, 'Then work for it.' They both come from the same origins, so why did one 'escape' and not the other? In the end, though, neither character is as clear-cut as they initially seem. Pat turns out to have a heart after all, while Margaret starts to stand up for herself, just as Wood did after her early, faltering steps in show business, when she realised that if she said 'no' often enough, people would start to say 'yes' to her. She was not Pat or Margaret, but both. She was as famous as one, as ordinary as the other.

Pat and Margaret seemed to be a way for Wood to exorcise a lot of ghosts, and in 1994 she sought further assistance to get to grips with the present and made it public that she had been seeing a therapist. She wouldn't reveal the true reasons for the visits, although speculation suggested that they had something to do with her guilt over not being there when her father had died. As ever, Wood was fairly dispassionate about her reasons for seeing an analyst, joking to the *Daily Mirror* that 'it was something to do of a Tuesday.' It certainly seemed out of character, if you thought Wood was like one of her characters – northerners didn't get depressed, they just got

OPPOSITE:

The Wood family en masse: Victoria, Geoffrey, Grace and Henry.

fed up and got on with life. But this was reality, not a BBC sketch. Therapy was basically a way of talking to someone who wasn't involved in her life and who would simply listen for fifty minutes a time. It was a simple financial transaction, but it seemed to do the trick. In the late '80s and early '90s, Wood had seemed anxious and tense. Even having children hadn't really settled her down. Maybe her attempts to juggle both her career and motherhood had compounded any pent-up emotional conflict. Whatever the reasons for the treatment, she seemed, as it were, to be finally 'out of the woods'. All she was worried about now was her public image. She was still as popular as ever; the public hadn't moved on to someone else, as she had always feared. But she did think they perceived her as somewhat cosy, and part of the thinking behind *Pat and Margaret* was to reveal this other side: 'Just because I look cosy doesn't mean I am,' she joked. As if to prove a point, in December 1994 she told a questioner that her favourite word was 'bum'. A very Victoria Wood way of being subversive.

That December Wood completed a momentous year with another Christmas Day show. After the spectacular skits of *All-Day Breakfast* in 1992, *Live In Your Own Home* was basically a chance for television viewers to see Wood's all-conquering stand-up act. Having broken box-office records around the country, one might have thought that there were few people who hadn't seen the show. It also marked the TV appearance of some of Wood's most colourful characters. As Fattitude Madge, she addressed her aerobics group in a flowery leotard: 'The Friday night low-impact class for fatties with attitude'; In the sketch *Toupee Time*, Charlene offered new tips on synthetic hair and read viewers' letters about old wigs: 'One in particular has interesting historical associations as it was blown off during the State Opening of Parliament, 1958.' The character Madeline was a slight return to Lorraine, the hairdresser who had fled the TV studios during *Over To Pam*, except that Madeline was a distinctly northern cousin, with a nice line in gossip with her clients: 'By the time she was twenty-one, she was smoking mentholated cigarillos and getting engaged to goalkeepers.' One way or another, everyone who was anyone got a chunk of Victoria Wood in 1994.

OPPOSITE:
The book of the film that nearly never was – fortunately the BBC stepped in when LWT seemed to opt out.

6

'Victoria and Albert'

In March 1995 the BBC's Comic Relief Night *screened Victoria Wood's latest attempt to help raise consciousnesses and money. Following her rather embarrassing record in 1991, this had more integrity and more success as she followed in the footsteps of Lenny Henry and Billy Connolly and travelled to Africa to film an in-depth, not very humorous, report. She visited the drought-blighted village of Chivi in Zimbabwe and spent a week with an African family there, becoming involved with a local project to save water. She had difficulties when they asked her to dance but no trouble helping out when it came to milking the cows: 'Having breast-fed my two kids for so long, it was a bit similar,' she suggested. Wood, who had been pretty hopeless when it came to maintenance on her Highgate home, now showed herself to be pretty hardy when it came to making drainpipes out of clay. She dug troughs and joined in with the weeding in temperatures of up to 100 degrees.*

OPPOSITE:
A smile for the lens but Wood still prefers to hide behind her trusty piano.

**Very glamorous:
In the '90s Wood's
femininity finally
emerged.**

OPPOSITE:
**Unwinding after a hard
day at t'laughter mill.**

It seemed slightly out of character for Victoria Wood to be up to her knees in dust, but as she entered her forties she was becoming more and more concerned about the environment and political issues. Asked whether she would consider having more children, she sounded more like *Jude the Obscure* than one of Britain's funniest comics when she said she doubted it because she wasn't sure if it was right to bring more people into a country that was filthy and already so overcrowded.

ABOVE:
**Another do,
another award.**

Nevertheless, she still felt uncomfortable about the idea of Victoria Wood as a spokesperson for a generation, although she did acknowledge in *She* that she had a very specific relationship with her audience: 'We're talking about the same sort of thing. But I'm the one actually saying it.' But Wood was more likely to be referring here to the pros and cons of Claire Rayner advertising the latest winged sanitary towels than the Tory Party's latest policies on education, crime and the environment.

Wood described herself as a Labour supporter with strong views but still didn't consider herself to be a political comic – although on-stage she did use politics to illustrate Britain as a country riddled with non-committal. For instance, whereas in Romania they had a revolution to oust Ceauscescu, Wood suggested that in Britain protesters would have merely written letters to *Points of View*.

She was also reluctant to align herself with the new wave of female comics. Now more confidant of her status, she said she admired Ruby Wax and Jennifer Saunders and even socialised with Dawn French when their hectic schedules allowed it, but she didn't consider herself to be in the vanguard of some kind of militant women-in-comedy platoon. She obviously had her doubts about the anger that swept through much of the Ben Elton-led comedy of the 1980s. In one interview she went as far as to suggest that the political comedy of that decade had been a fad which was now finished. Wood seemed more in tune with someone like John Betjeman, a man with obvious opinions about the state of the nation but who would still be polishing the rust off his bicycle handlebars even as others were manning the

ABOVE:
**John Betjeman:
Poet Laureate who,
like Wood, hid his
militant side beneath
a rapier-like wit.**

barricades. Wood simply takes a look at life around her, feeds the information through her 'barmy filter' and comes out with a hilarious take on reality.

Success, Wood felt, hadn't changed her. She and Geoffrey Durham had a nice house and a nice car, but she was still prudent about money when it came to buying outfits for the children: 'Grace's clothes come from Woolworths and Henry just wears hers. Though not every boy suits a dress.'

Wood's fans were a mixed blessing. There was definitely something strange about a group of adults – mostly, it had to be said, women – who would gather together to recite the dialogue from *Acorn Antiques*. The best thing about her acolytes was an endless supply of woolly jumpers.

As 1996 emerged Victoria Wood continued to take on a heavy workload. She somehow found time to joke about her predicament: 'Perhaps I should franchise myself. Like The Body Shop.' By now Geoffrey Durham had officially retired The Great Soprendo. He still performed as a magician under his own name and regularly appeared as the spelling expert on the day-time Channel Four quiz *Countdown* (which probably explains why Wood doesn't satirise day-time game shows very often), but he was always able to help out with the children if his wife needed to work away from home. While she continued to write in Highgate, working on both a stage play and a sitcom, jobs came in and took her away from time to time. She put in an appearance as a tea lady in Terry Jones's *Wind in the Willows*, which united all the surviving members of *Monty Python* for the first time in over a decade. Wood could have compared notes with John Cleese – also the child of a suburban man in insurance, also from a provincial town, also extremely funny, also of unusual physical

'If you don't change
as you get older,
you become a fossil'

LEFT:
**Dashing off while
Geoffrey is at home
holding the babies.**

proportions. Cleese was an only child, while Wood's siblings were much older – the nearest thing to being an only child. Cleese, like Wood, was hugely successful. And also someone who, despite the outward appearance of a charmed life, had sought recourse to therapy over the years. The only thing Cleese had achieved that Wood hadn't was success in America. She had never been there and was keen to pursue her career Stateside, as long as she could find the right vehicle, something of a challenge for someone with an identity that wasn't merely English but distinctly regional. Alexei Sayle, Peter Cook and Billy Connolly had all tried to break into the American sitcom market without becoming superstars. If Wood were ever to succeed where they had failed that would be a real mark of greatness.

In interviews Wood didn't seem to suggest that she was riddled with any more anxieties than the average performer. She had dreams about appearing on-stage without any lines, saying nonsense and not knowing when to start, but then again, what performer hasn't? Maybe it is in the nature of the performing arts, and comedy in particular, which depends so much on a direct and instant response, that a person has to be slightly mad, or certainly slightly neurotic, to want to do it in the first place. Two years on from opening up about therapy, Wood seemed more than able to dissemble and trivialise something that was obviously important to her, joking that counselling was 'like polishing your shoes, only it costs more' and later, 'like tidying your knicker drawer'. Yet her treatment had clearly had profound effects. Throughout her life she had been body conscious, comparing her shape first to her thinner sisters, then to her willowy contemporaries at Birmingham University. Was it merely a coincidence that she ended up marrying someone who was similarly overweight? In the early years she had used her own physique in her comedy to get the abuse in before the hecklers did. She once asked on-stage why fat girls were always bridesmaids. Just because it was funny and observant didn't mean that it wasn't also a pointed reference to her own sense of isolation.

The therapy seemed to coincide with the weight loss; it certainly boosted her confidence about her self-image. She had always suffered from the classic comedian's neurosis – wanting to be liked. For a lot of her adult life she certainly had been, and she had seven BAFTA Awards around the house to prove it, but she seemed reluctant to admit it. Now she felt better about herself than ever. She had always said that she never wore skirts, but in 1996, for the first time since her schooldays, she was photographed in a skirt.

Wood can be said to be a classic 'comedian's comedian'. Shy and retiring, yet able to hold a packed house in the palm of their hand. It has always seemed odd that a self-confessed shy person can actually get up and speak in front of 5,000 people.

Wood is not alone in being able to do this – there are countless, cripplingly shy actors, many with stutters, who are perfectly articulate in public – but in April 1996 she did come up with a spot of self-analysis in *OK Magazine* which seemed to explain the logic behind this strange behavioural phenomenon: 'I think a lot of shy people are really egomaniacs who haven't actually found a way to communicate with people, so they choose circumstances where they are in control and can set the agenda. Performing is the perfect job for a shy person. They can say exactly what they want to say whereas in a social situation they might be clumsy or tongue-tied. I am not very adept at parties, but put me on the stage of the Albert Hall and I can cope.'

'Perhaps I should franchise myself. Like The Body Shop'

She was due for another long run at the Royal Albert Hall in the autumn, but before then she road-tested her new show, nipping out of Highgate on Sunday nights in the spring to test the new material in nearby towns such as Watford and High Wycombe, but getting home in time to watch the Shopping Channel and QVC, programmes that made terrestrial cheap television seem like Spielberg. She even confessed to having bought a jewellery box from one of the programmes, though when it arrived she was disappointed with it and gave it to Geoffrey, who kept some of his smaller magic tricks in it.

Maybe now she is about to become that political animal she always shied away from. She even acknowledged the changes taking place in a *Guardian* interview when she said, 'If you don't change as you get older, you become a fossil.'

By the time autumn swung around, a publicity agent with second sight and a golden mobile phone couldn't have raised Victoria Wood's profile as high as it got. In September she presented a BBC2 *Great Railway Journeys* documentary, was the subject of an LWT *South Bank Show* and started another box-office smashing residency at the Royal Albert Hall. This three-pronged PR coup pushed Wood firmly into the limelight and, more importantly, showcased a new image.

The *Great Railway Journeys* was perhaps the most startling of all. Not surprisingly Wood had turned down offers to go to Mexico and Uruguay in favour of a trip round Britain from 'Crewe to Crewe'. Viewers turned on expecting the usual assortment of cake references and cuppas, and while they got those, they also got a venomous diatribe against the state of British Rail. Wood was not nostalgic for the old days, which just made her think of formica tables and daily trips to Manchester, but neither did she like the current state of affairs, with the networks being broken up, small services being killed off and the arteries of tourist routes being clogged up

by senior citizens. It left a sour taste, but was undoubtedly an impassioned, heartfelt piece. At one point she came across a station which boasted a Christian bookshop. She laid into this verbally, suggesting that the rubber hippos on sale were probably made by a four year old in Taiwan who may well have been manacled to a workbench at the time. She was no less charitable about some of the waiting rooms: 'The smell of urine is available on Ceefax.'

With violinist Yehudi Menuhin
and a cake in the shape of the
Albert Hall – her second home
when it comes to performing.

Princess Diana: press
rumours suggested she wanted
to discuss eating disorders
and therapy with Wood.

The *South Bank Show* profile showed Wood preparing for the tour of her new show. It revealed her to be thoughtful and not particularly funny. It was as if comedy was just a job of work for her – which, of course, it was. But it was one that she took extremely seriously. If the slightest thing was wrong in rehearsals she would change it, right up to showtime. This probably explains how, by the time the show reached the Royal Albert Hall it was a spectacular success, two-and-a-half hours of solo hilarity, the kind of high-laugh-ratio very few contemporary British comics, maybe only Ben Elton or Billy Connolly, could dream of matching.

The jokes poured forth and kept the audience – men, women, youngsters, oldsters – smiling for the duration. If there was a lull it came during the musical interludes, which Wood has never quite shaken off. Only a number about the fact that she wasn't allowed to say 'wanker' any more made it worth heaving the piano on to the stage at all.

It was a show that mixed the predictable with the shocking. Even before she opened her mouth she kicked things off with a poke at royalty, spoofing Princess Diana's droopy-eyed paparazzi image in the tour programme. (This could just have been a retort to gossip column suggestions that Princess Diana had currently wanted to befriend Victoria; the theory was that because Victoria had had therapy and a weight problem they would both have plenty in common to talk about.) The on-stage material continued to knock people who were in the public eye, alongside domestic and social scenarios which are perennially ripe for comedy. Ken Barlow made his regular appearance as a celebrity victim of one of Wood's asides; unbearable family Christmases was a well-worn routine; colonic irrigation and cellulite got a look-in; foreplay was like beefburgers – 'three minutes on each side'.

For an encore she did her leotard-clad aerobics teacher from the Fattitude sketch. The late Jack Tinker called her 'a national treasure', and he was spot on. But add 'unique' to that honour, too. How many other national treasures have stood up in front of 5,000 people and discussed how their pubic hair is turning into a rockery plant: 'spreading, joining, clumping up'. She was only forty-three and yet ageing seemed to have become a preoccupation. In one song she sang about going straight from '10CC to HRT, turning left at Elton John'.

Even when the material fell back on old faithfuls, new twists turned it into strong stuff. Wood suggested using a seventeen-year-old tampon as an anti-mugging device – if you stuffed it up their nose the assailant might die of toxic shock syndrome.

OPPOSITE:

Gagging for it: Wood lets rip.

By the end of 1996, Victoria Wood had brought smiles to the faces of thousands of fans all over the United Kingdom. For the little girl who never quite fitted in, it still didn't seem to be enough.

A new tour was arranged for the spring of 1997, when she would return to the scenes of some of her greatest live triumphs by popular demand. As she had said many years earlier, it was 'live' that she came 'alive'. It was live where she could control the situation. It was live where she could really be herself.

Except that Victoria Wood on-stage isn't the real Victoria Wood. Live comedy is all about wearing a mask. Perhaps that is part of the reason why Wood is disturbed by the fans who take things too far and model themselves on her. They think they will then have lives like Victoria Wood when in fact they seem blissfully unaware that they are just donning a yellow beret or a Mrs Overall hairnet.

No one, of course, could ever be another Victoria Wood. She has carved out her career with the ruthless discipline of a master tactician, overcoming every obstacle that has appeared in front of her. Maybe she also had the help of a few conjuring tricks, taught by her husband Geoffrey Durham, because she has certainly worked miracles. In one of her songs, Wood suggests that 'Life was planned by a committee while the clever ones had popped out to the lav.' Her own early professional struggle bears this out, but then again, a less bumpy ride might not have resulted in such a well-rounded performer.

There will be more comedians in the future. Some may even be funnier than Victoria Wood. But none will have her voice, share her spirit, or have such a rapport with their audience. In being ordinary, and connecting with her public, Victoria Wood has become extraordinary, a one-in-a-million mirth-maker. The best comedians stand alone.

ABOVE:
Content at last: two decades on from
New Faces, Wood can smile, having
conquered the small screen and the
big stage. But what next?

Acknowledgements

Many thanks to everyone too humorous to mention who assisted me in the compilation of this book. In particular many thanks to my indulgent employers *Time Out* and to Cath, Lily and Florence, who stayed out of my way when necessary and laughed at Victoria's jokes in all the right places when they were around.

Photographic Credits

All Action Pictures
Pages 93, 95.

Big Pictures
Pages 9, 45, 61, 62, 67, 77, 102.

Camera Press Ltd.
Pages 35, 42, 47, 52, 69, 74, 80, 89, 96, 97.

Capital Pictures
Pages 2, 20, 22, 25, 33, 53, 65, 72, 86, 101, 105.

Crucible Studio Theatre, Sheffield
Pages 13, 17.

Frank Spooner Pictures Ltd.
Page 85

JS Library International
Page 106.

London Features International
Pages 23, 44.

Mirror Syndication
Pages 7, 8, 31, 41, 79, 81.

PA News Photo Library
Pages 57, 60.

Pappix UK
Page 107.

Retna Pictures Ltd.
Pages 14, 32.

Rex Features Ltd.
Pages 10, 16, 19, 24, 27, 28, 30, 58, 68, 73, 99.

Scope Features
Pages 12, 26, 29, 38/39, 43, 46, 49, 50, 54, 64, 76, 82, 100, 110, 111.

Universal Pictorial Press & Agency Ltd.
Pages 83, 90.